The Five Decisions

That Can

Transform Your Life Forever

A.K. Spencer

Inspirit Books

To my loving mother, Adela, who inspires me to seek out my happiness, live life to its fullest, and more importantly, taught me that anything is possible.

Acknowledgments

"Let no one seek his own, but each the other's well being."
~ 1 Corinthians 10:24

At some point in the course of our lifetime, we realize that we have the power. Prior to this realization, we may spend much of our time waiting for things to happen to us, or reacting to the people that surround us or events that occur in our lives. When we awaken to the reality that, unlike a feather floating on a breeze at the whim of any gust of wind that may come along to determine where we land, we have the power. We have always had the power to control our life experience and determine our own fate, in spite of the things that may happen to us and over which we do not have control.

I am grateful for the life experiences I have had. Both the experiences resulting from things over which I had no control, as well as for those life experiences I created knowingly and unknowingly through thoughts, words, or actions.

I am also thankful for those people who are part of my life and who support me unconditionally. They are my family and friends. Thanks to all who helped to bring this project to fruition: my husband Spencer Fallgatter, my children Lexi Fallgatter and Kristian Fallgatter; my siblings Marisa Espinoza, Diane Espinoza, and Manny Espinoza. Thanks to my parents, Manuel and Adela, for raising us with love and care, and for their constant support. Thanks also to my nephews Devon Grijalva and David Grijalva, my friends Joanne Stark, Joe Fernandez, Eadie Rudder, and my sister-in-law Juleann Fallgatter. I know that I am blessed.

Table of Contents

INTRODUCTION

I ASKED, HE ANSWERED

The idea for this book came to me on a lovely spring morning in March of 2009. While having lunch with my friend Jenna[1], who had recently been informed that she had a heart condition that would require surgery, we decided we would take the afternoon to see a movie. However, she had planned to go to the chapel nearby to pray and meditate, and she asked if I would mind accompanying her there before going to the movie. After entering the chapel and taking a seat in one of the pews, I knelt on the kneeler and said a quick prayer then sat silently. It was then that a question came to mind. After the question, came an answer, followed by a series of questions and answers that took me by surprise.

Here's how it went:

Question: Why am I here Lord?
Answer: You are here to serve.

---

[1] Names of individuals have been changed in order to protect their privacy.

Question: How may I serve you Lord?
Answer: You may serve me by serving others.

Question: How may I serve others?
Answer: You may serve others by responding to their needs.

Question: How do I discover their needs?
Answer: You can discover their needs by looking within, for as a fellow human, you can relate to their plight. Look within.

The event was quick and surreal. I did not know what to make of the experience, nor did I know what to do with the information. In the course of the weeks that followed, I meditated in hopes of gaining more information or direction. At some point soon thereafter, I realized the direction had been given and was clear. Look within. So, I did.

In examining my own life, I discovered the following:

- Throughout my life, I have occasionally felt lost and unsure of my purpose and direction.

- In spite of those feelings, I managed in many ways to be successful on my own terms.
- Success in life is not a final destination, but an evolutionary process through which our souls experience growth.
- In every success I have experienced, certain factors were consistently present and were common threads to achievement. I felt the need to share them, and refer to these factors as:

THE FIVE DECISIONS

This book explains THE FIVE DECISIONS that can change your life for the better. There are no new or startling revelations or information with which you are unfamiliar. Others have written about some of these decisions or aspects of them. Indeed, I have read many a self-help book by the greats, such as Dyer, Osteen, Williamson, Chopra, Hay, Robbins, and others. They have not been addressed, however, in the manner in which they are presented here. There are other factors that may, of course, add to, enhance, or change your life. In staying true to my vision, however, I chose to focus strictly on THE FIVE DECISIONS that will have, if

3

consistently applied together, the greatest impact. Each of THE FIVE DECISIONS is explained in detail in the chapters included in each of the sections which follow this Introduction.

WHY NOW?

A while back, I authored a book in which I wrote:

> *In the course of a lifetime, there are many people who come into and go out of our lives. Some are steadfast in their presence, others fleeting. Each serves a particular purpose or teaches a particular lesson. Those people – our loved ones, family members, friends, and even perfect strangers – leave distinct imprints on the pages in the book of our souls.*[2]

I am a strong proponent of the idea that everything happens for a reason, and that people and things come into our lives to serve a purpose. Large or small, there is a lesson we are intended to

---

[2] Excerpted from "The Most Important Letter You Will Ever Write." Inspirit Books, LLC, 2006

learn from them, or they from us. For reasons unknown to me, and possibly to you as well, you have been called to read this book. My wish is that this book will serve to move you toward the things you want to achieve, and thereby, enhance your life experience.

DECISION I

DECIDE THAT YOU ARE RESPONSIBLE AND IN CONTROL

Chapter 1

YOU ARE WORTHY

If you are reading this book, one thing is for certain - there is hope in your heart; hope and desire for a life better than the life you are now living. This alone speaks volumes about the person that you are and your approach to living.

It is important to realize that although most of us strive to be happy and successful, we don't necessarily have a sense of what, exactly, that means to us. In addition, though we may want and seek happiness and success, there might be a part of us that believes that (for whatever reason) we do not deserve to be happy, nor that we have what it takes to be successful. And that is precisely the problem. What you believe about anything is exactly what you will experience. If somewhere, deep within yourself, you believe that you can never be happy – you're absolutely correct. What you believe becomes your reality. Thus, no matter how diligent your efforts to find happiness and success, they will not be yours. This means that you must carefully examine, identify, and change both your core beliefs and your thoughts as a first step, in order to have what has eluded you thus far.

Perhaps you have been waiting for permission to be happy or were never told that you deserve it. In fact, you may have heard and believe quite the opposite. Messages we may have heard as youngsters from parents, teachers, and others seep into our minds and may stay with us well into adulthood. Although we all have specific lessons we must learn during our lifetime, which will ultimately contribute to the growth of our souls, that does not mean that we are not intended or not destined to lead happy and fulfilled lives. Indeed, we were put on this earth for that purpose. However, since happiness is individual, you must determine for yourself what constitutes happiness and bring it into your life.

One reason people are unhappy and unsuccessful may be because they have not been true to themselves and are living lives that do not reflect who they really are. They're doing things they are not passionate about. Many live their lives to meet expectations of others, such as parents, spouses, siblings, teachers, and coaches.

As previously noted, the primary reason a person's life is what it is today, is because of their beliefs. Their beliefs, and the thoughts and actions associated with those beliefs, have led them to create the life they lead. As noted, what you believe about anything and everything, and the thoughts associated with your beliefs have brought about what you are now experiencing. Consequently, changing your life means changing what you believe, and also what you think about regularly.

Some people believe that they deserve whatever they get because they have made mistakes in the past. If you feel this way, it is high time you let go of the past and forgive yourself. Nobody judges us more harshly than we do ourselves. But, focusing on the past prevents us from moving forward. We get trapped reliving the feelings of guilt instead of taking the intended lesson and moving on. Therefore, whatever your mistakes, forgive yourself and be thankful for the experience of learning something that is likely to serve a positive purpose now and in the future.

In addition, there is a general belief that life is supposed to be hard. Society teaches us that anything worth having necessarily entails difficulty or hardship. This attitude is reflected in the phrase frequently used in reference to sports and fitness: "no pain, no gain." However, pain does not necessarily equal gain, and may even result in injury. In fact, it may signal that you are going about what you are doing in the wrong way. Life does not have to be hard. Believing otherwise is self-defeating and may also be self-fulfilling.

Since our belief system is the foundation upon which we build our lives, if your life has not been what you hoped it would be, it's time to examine and perhaps challenge and change your beliefs. To do so, however, you must determine which beliefs are getting in the way and keeping you from getting where you want to go.

WHAT DO YOU BELIEVE?

I truly believe in the statement "you are what you think." More clearly stated, you are (and your life experience is) what you think about, believe in, and the things on which you focus your attention.

I can personally attest to this concept. After college, I was admitted to law school. After completing law school, I prepared to take the state bar exam which is required in order to be licensed to practice law in the state. The exam, at the time, was a comprehensive two-day exam consisting of one day of essay questions and one day of multiple-choice questions across several areas of law. In preparation for the exam, many law school grads (or soon to be grads) participate in review courses to prepare themselves. However, in spite of studying diligently over the course of several months, and participating in a review course in preparation for the exam, I convinced myself (and truly believed) that I could not, and would not pass the exam. Those highly negative thoughts remained with me during the next failed attempts to pass. They were at the forefront of my mind when preparing to take the exam and remained my focus throughout my preparation. "You are going to fail. There is no way you will pass. This is a hard exam and the pass rate is not that great." In addition, and possibly related to these thoughts was the fact that I had suffered from severe exam anxiety throughout law school, and it was clearly still with me.

As a result of the constant barrage of negative thoughts, my self-confidence and self-esteem were extremely low. I questioned whether I should keep trying, whether I would ever pass, and also questioned my choice of career path. At some point during that very difficult time, I picked up a book by Anthony Robbins. That book helped me to realize the error of my ways, to question my thinking, and thereby change my experience. I began to pay close attention to what I was thinking, saying, and doing. I quickly realized that my beliefs and self-talk were doing me in. My constant focus on failure was not only self-defeating, but indeed, self-fulfilling. Once I realized that I was creating the reality of failing, I promptly decided to change my thinking, and started to do just that. As a result, I passed the exam and became a member of the bar. To be clear, <u>this was a process</u>. This did not happen overnight and there was nothing miraculous or magical about what happened. I chose to acknowledge my limiting beliefs as being the problem, and took steps to change my experience and the outcome.

What are your beliefs? Take a moment to think about and answer the following questions and examine your responses:

- What do you believe about happiness?
- What do you believe about success?
- What do you believe about your past mistakes?

Are your beliefs supporting or hindering your ability to be happy and successful? If they are not supporting you, it is time to . . .

Chapter 2

MANAGE YOUR THOUGHTS, CONTROL YOUR LIFE

SUCCESS IS ALL ABOUT YOU

In this life, there are no Fairy Godmothers or other people or sources outside of ourselves that we can rely on to make our dreams come true. Whether you are happy or unhappy with your current status or circumstances in life, there is only one person who can and must take full responsibility for it, and that person is you.

Only you have the power to decide what you want. Only you know the right thing to do. Only you can decide where to focus your attention, and thus, only you can take action to make your life what you want it to be. Although you may not have control over the actions of others or of outside forces or events, you do have control over your reactions to those people or events.

With time, we gain experience. With experience comes wisdom. If you think about where you are now, and think back to thoughts you had, decisions you made, and actions you took in the past, you can be sure that those thoughts, decisions and actions got you where you are today. In planning for success, it is important to consider your past experience and use it as a guide in directing the path that will lead you where you want to go. Use both your experiences and the wisdom gained from those experiences to help you achieve the success that you seek.

CHANGING YOUR MIND

I once heard a speaker say "change your attitude, change your life." I don't remember where I was or who uttered those words, but they remained with me and have had a significant impact on how I live my life. I did not know exactly what it meant at the time, but I have since come to learn the importance of both thoughts and attitude in living happily. Changing your attitude means changing your thinking. Changing my attitude by controlling my thoughts has led to many of my personal achievements, and has also seen me though some of the most difficult times in my life.

The truth is that we often don't realize the impact our thoughts have on how we live. What we say to ourselves, both in our thoughts and aloud, has an effect on the way we feel, our perspective, and is directly reflected in the way we live. You've heard the expression "you are what you eat." Well, "you are what you think" too. Some food for thought: The life you lead today is a direct result of the thoughts and beliefs you have had in the recent past. What your life is in the future will be determined by your thoughts and beliefs of the present. Thus, it is important to pay attention to, monitor, and control what you are thinking.

TAKING CONTROL

As previously noted, at some point in life, we realize that (for the most part) we have absolutely no control over other people or over events that may take place in our lives. This is especially true when we feel victimized, helpless, hopeless, or out of control. What we may sometimes fail to remember is that we do have the sole power to control our OWN emotions. How we react to or whether the events or the actions of others affect us is completely within our power.

Too often in life we tend to shift blame or responsibility for our emotions to someone else. They made us feel angry or sad. The reality is that we create those emotions, and the responsibility as to how we feel, what we think, and how we react falls squarely on our shoulders. Failure to recognize this and to let other people or events dictate how you feel, think, or react is to completely relinquish control of your life to unknown forces.

Therefore, one of the first steps toward changing your life for the better is to willingly accept that responsibility. The way to achieve this is to change your attitude by changing the way in which you evaluate the behavior of others and events that occur in your life. Taking control of your emotions and attitude means that you are in total control of your own world.

WHAT ARE YOU LOOKING AT?

If the manner in which we evaluate people or things that happen around us causes us to be unhappy, then we have the power to change it. This is called changing or gaining perspective. One way to do it is to recognize that everything is not about us. If a person makes a rude or hurtful comment, we may ask ourselves what we did to cause that person to treat us that way, when, in fact, it may have nothing at all to do with us. Indeed, another person's behavior is usually all about them. My mother uses the expression (in Spanish) "cada mente es un mundo," which loosely translates to "every mind is a world of it's own." It means that every person has their own truth, their own reality, and thus, their own perspective. So if another person conducts himself in a manner that is offensive to you – don't take it personally and let it go. Perhaps the person that was rude to you is having a bad day. Maybe they were late for work, received a speeding ticket on the way there, and were chewed out by their supervisor once they arrived. This does not, of course, excuse their attitude and/or rudeness toward you. It is important to realize, however, that another person's conduct is likely based on whatever is happening with them, not necessarily something you did. It is all about their perspective, their worry, their fears, and their insecurities. Therefore, you can decide not to be offended by them and to let it go.

In late 1999 and early 2000, I was working for a state government agency. Right around the middle of the second year of employment, the division I worked in was restructured. My supervisor combined two units into one. This change increased my duties and the number of staff I supervised. I was now managing two departments instead of one. As a result, I requested and received a change in title and an increase in pay. The news of the change was not received well by three colleagues who had been in their positions longer than I had been in mine. I had previously been one level below their titles, and the change put me one level above their titles. They were hopping mad. During that same period, my supervisor who was highly regarded on a national level, considered a standout in the field, and highly sought after, was recruited by a state agency in another state. Shortly thereafter, the new supervisor held a meeting with the entire division staff. At the time, only a few weeks had passed, and the tension was still thick in the office. It was clear to me that my colleagues remained very unhappy. During the meeting, one of my colleagues, Judee, behaved appallingly. She berated me and made derogatory comments regarding our former supervisor in front of the group. As an ardent supporter of professionalism and diplomacy, I was flabbergasted at her behavior. I had never seen and could not imagine anyone behaving in such a rude and unprofessional manner. Although this created a rift within the department, and upset me initially, I later realized that the outburst was all about her, not me. Judee felt slighted, and insecure. It is possible that I may very well have felt similarly had I been in her position. Nevertheless, I would never treat anyone the way she treated me, regardless of how I felt. Still, titles and salaries are a hot button issue. The identities of some people are completely tied to their titles and how much they earn. That seemed to be the case with Judee. Once I realized this by changing my perspective, I was able to let go of it and move on.

CHECK YOUR ATTITUDE

Is your attitude self-defeating? Although you may consider yourself to be a person with a positive attitude, you may need to make a conscious effort to monitor what you are thinking and saying to yourself and to others. Though some people seem to take pleasure in complaining about things, constantly focusing on the negative aspects of anything accomplishes nothing and detracts from our ability to focus on what is good and how we can get more of it.

I have always considered myself to be an inordinately positive and optimistic person. I remember that my upbeat personality and positive outlook irked as least one person. When I was in my early twenties working as a law clerk at a law firm, I happily walked into the office one afternoon and cheerfully greeted a fellow student/co-worker. She grimaced and informed me that it annoyed her that I was always smiling and happy. Surprised at first, I brushed off the comment and thought she just might be having a bad day. Nobody is immune to having a bad day, or a bad attitude or perspective. I was reminded of this in a recent conversation with my teenage daughter. She pointed out that the comments I was making were critical and negative. Indeed, they were. Over time, we may become somewhat jaded. We may tend to look for what is wrong, instead of what is right. Doing so, however, accomplishes nothing, except to make us (or others) feel bad and to perpetuate a negative state of mind.

THE COMPANY YOU KEEP

If you've ever been around anyone who seems to constantly focus on the negative (and it is likely you have been at some point in your life) you know it can be exhausting. Despite any efforts you may make to control your own emotions and attitudes, if you are surrounded by negative people they will have a negative impact on you. On the other hand, surrounding yourself with people who have a positive outlook on life is uplifting, and can help you move forward. To that end, it is important to create a network of people around you who have a positive outlook, who love you, care about what you are doing, and support you unconditionally. Also important, is having at least one person in your life who is enthusiastic about life. Enthusiasm and excitement for living can be highly contagious. Unfortunately, so can a negative outlook.

When I was in college, I became friends with a girl named Nadia. Although she was highly intelligent and fun-loving, I soon discovered that Nadia was a chronic complainer and gossip. Nearly every conversation I had with her consisted of problems, complaints, and negative talk about others. In spite of my efforts to counter the negativity, at some point during our two year friendship, I concluded that my efforts were wasted. I would leave conversations with her feeling physically and emotionally drained, and in a bad frame of mind. This was taking a toll on my outlook, and I decided to distance myself from Nadia. It took me some time, but I finally realized that despite whatever benefits there were in maintaining the friendship, those were outweighed by the detrimental impact of the constant bombardment of negativity. I later broke off the friendship altogether. It was a difficult decision, but one which I felt was in my best interest in the end.

In contrast, I have also met people who have the ability to immediately uplift the mood in any environment. Ada, a former co-worker, is a perfect example of someone who could instantly change the atmosphere in a room just by walking into it. While working as a program administrator at a private university, I met Ada. She was a graduate student who had been hired to work as a tutor. While sitting at my desk, I could hear that someone had entered the room. Before she even spoke, I could sense a change of energy in the room. I then heard Ada introduce herself to another co-worker and her voice had a palpable uplifting energy to it. As I got to know Ada better, I was constantly amazed at how her whole being seemed always to be bursting with positivity. She consistently looked for and found the upside to any problem or situation, and had a strong belief that something good came out of any problem or challenge. In talking to Ada one day, she told me the story of how just a few years earlier, at the age of eighteen, she had been in a serious car accident on the highway and had been paralyzed. The prognosis for her recovery and regaining use of her legs was not good. She said that, at the time, she believed she would walk again regardless of what the doctors were telling her. Throughout the ordeal, she believed she would make a full recovery, and over time, she did. Ada said that although she would not wish it on her worst enemy, if she had to live through it again, she would. She felt that she was ultimately a better person because of that painful experience.

NOT TO WORRY

Although we cannot avoid it completely, it's important to know that worry is a form of negativity. In addition to affecting our general mood and demeanor, worry, and the stress associated with worry, can negatively impact our physical and emotional well-being. Thus, it makes sense that the less we worry, the better off we are.

To worry is to experience concern or anxiety over something that has either already happened, or which we anticipate will happen. The trouble is that so much of the time we spend worrying is wasted on things that we either have no control over or which may never actually happen. Since the dreaded outcome is not certain, we should try to refrain from worrying about it. This philosophy is reflected in the phrase, "I'll cross that bridge when I come to it." This, however, is much easier said than done.

Because many of the things we worry about do not involve life or death situations (i.e. failing an exam, breaking up with someone, not meeting a deadline), one way to address the issue is by answering the following questions:

- What is the worst that can happen?
- If the worst were to happen, how would I deal with it; what are my options?

The answers may not be perfect or to your complete satisfaction, but you are certain to feel better because you, at the very least, have a plan of action if the worst does happen. By having a plan, you have faced the unknown and can stop worrying about it.

The key is to avoid being distracted by limiting thoughts, emotions, a negative attitude and/or worry. The idea is to let happiness and peace of mind become a daily ritual and normal state. A happy and peaceful mind can focus on making dreams a reality.

DECIDE

Before you go to the next page, decide to:

- Examine your beliefs, identify and change the beliefs that are impeding your success.
- Take full responsibility for your attitude, emotions, and keep them in check.
- In each situation, ask: Is my attitude serving me well?
- Choose your friends wisely. Are the people you surround yourself with and spend time with serving a beneficial purpose in your life or are you, in theirs?
- Avoid worry by having a plan of action in the event whatever you are worried about occurs.

DECISION II

DECIDE PRECISELY WHAT YOU WANT

Chapter 3

FIND YOUR HAPPINESS

DO IT NOW

Don't put off for another life what you could accomplish in this one. If you are waiting for happiness to somehow magically appear in your life, you have a long wait ahead of you. If you are relying on someone else to make you happy, you have misplaced your trust. The only person who can make you happy, is you. And if you truly want it, you must seek it out with relentless fervor. If you believe it's too late to be happy, know this: Until you are dead, it is NEVER TOO LATE.

WHAT, EXACTLY, DO YOU WANT?

The answer to the question "what constitutes happiness" is unique to every person. Most people know exactly and can describe in great detail what they <u>don't</u> want based upon what they have previously or are currently experiencing in life. However, most people can tell you, in only general terms, what would make them happy (i.e. more money, a bigger home, a better job, and even more money), and therein lies the problem. If what you want can be described by you solely in terms that are vague and unclear, you will not get it. One of the keys to getting what you want is <u>precision</u>. You must have a clear and exact vision of what it is you want. You must be able to envision it (touch it and feel it, and see it) in your own mind, as if it already exists. In addition, you must be completely convinced (have faith and certainty) that you will be successful in getting it.

IN SEARCH OF THE GOOD LIFE

Many people equate living the good life with living large: having a large home or a large bank account. However, although they may make life easier, it is often said that material things will not make you happy or happier in the long run. Living the life you want means living and enjoying your life. To me, it means being surrounded by the people and things I love, and doing those things that make me happy.   One of the best things you can do for yourself in this lifetime is to find out what you love to do and do it. Doing what you love means to live passionately.   Each day is filled with the excitement and satisfaction of knowing your time will be spent doing what you love most, instead of dreading getting out of bed and going to work. It is possible, however, that you may not have yet found a way to do what you love to generate income. If this is the case for you, the next chapter may help you to discover your passion.

Chapter 4

DISCOVER YOUR PASSION

DO WHAT YOU LOVE

Several years ago, I was leaving a good paying position doing work I liked to stay at home with my two young children. The week before I left, I was having a conversation with Sandy, a colleague, who asked, "If you weren't doing this kind of work, what would you most like to be doing?" With barely a pause to ponder the question, I quickly replied: "I think I'd be a writer." I'd always wanted to write, and had indeed done some writing, but had never really made time to pursue it professionally. The reason is that although I knew I was passionate about writing very early on, I considered it only a hobby, and not a possible career. Instead, I spent my time up until then preparing for a career in a field I thought I ought to go into, and later in a career in which I was only mildly content. As a going away gift, Sandy gave me a book on writing and publishing. It was one of the best gifts I have ever received, as it was instrumental in re-directing my path and my focus in life. Although my life did not change overnight, I began researching and reading everything I could find regarding writing and publishing. I read many books, subscribed to websites, enrolled in workshops, joined writing groups, and learned as much as I could about all of the various aspects of writing and publishing. When I was ready, I began to write. Doing so was not a challenge. In fact, I would become so enthralled in what I was doing, I felt as if time would fly by every time I sat down to write. I was happy. I had discovered one of my great passions in life. Similarly, in the summer of 2004, I discovered a talent and passion for songwriting that seemed to appear out of the blue.

DISCOVERING YOUR DESTINY

What do you love to do? You may know and you may be doing it already. What you love to do, of course, may not be limited to one thing. Thus, a better question is: What do you love doing most? If you are not quite sure, there are ways to discover it:

- Revisiting childhood dreams

As a young child, what did you enjoy doing most? What did you dream of growing up to become? Did you have a special talent and interest in something specific, such as animals, dancing, writing, singing, drawing, science, or playing baseball? Those talents displayed and interests developed at a young age may be indicators of a hidden or long lost passion you may want to explore further.

- Not so hidden talents

Are there things which you are inherently good at doing? What things were you good at doing as a child or in adolescence, that you continue to be good at as an adult? Have you developed special talents over time through either education or training and which you also enjoy doing? Being good at something does not mean you enjoy or are passionate about doing it. It is, however, a good place to start if you have not yet discovered your passion.

- Losing yourself

What do you get lost in while doing them? Think about the things you enjoy doing so much that you lose track of time while engaged in that activity. Being so focused and enjoying an activity so much that you lose track of time and things going on around you are indicators that you are passionate about that activity.

- Pursuing your interests

Being passionate about something and being interested in something are two different things. Passion refers to an ardent enthusiasm and thorough enjoyment of something. Thus, something that draws an intense positive emotional response is something about which you are passionate. An interest refers to something that may draw your attention, but about which you may not be passionate.

Although others may be able to help you discover or rediscover your passion, only you can know for certain the things about which you are passionate. Once you know what that is, you can move ahead with finding a way to live your passion every day.

DECIDE

Before you go to the next page, decide to:

- Act now to find your happiness
- Take the time to discover your passion if you do not already know what it is.

DECISION III

DECIDE TO PLAN AND TAKE ACTION

Chapter 5

THE PLAN

Over the course of the last three decades I have set many goals for things I wanted to accomplish in my lifetime; things I thought would make me a better and happier person. As happens to us all, some goals were achieved and others got lost in the shuffle of life.

In looking back on the goals I accomplished, I found some common threads:

1. I had a clear and precise vision of the goal(s) I wanted to accomplish.
2. I had an evolving plan as to how I was going to accomplish each goal.
3. I took action by following my plan, until I achieved my goal.
4. I had complete faith (certainty and belief) that I would accomplish my goal(s).
5. I spent time focusing on my goal daily by following the plan, and through meditation and visualization techniques.

This chapter addresses items 1 to 3 from the above list. Items 4 through 5 are covered in chapters that follow.

CREATING THE VISION

In prior chapters, we covered the importance of knowing exactly what you want and that, as such, precision of vision is key. If you are one of the many who can speak in detail about what you don't want in your life, but can only speak in general terms about your goals, it is essential to remedy that before moving ahead. In other words, your vision of what you want should be exceedingly clear to you. The precision of your vision will help you achieve it. This means that you must give some thought to what you want. You must, in your own mind, be able to see it clearly, touch it, and feel it as if it already exists. The vision needs to exist in your mind, before you can create the reality of it. As an example, a musician who wants to form a band and record an album needs to create a vision of that experience. He would need to, in his mind, see (visualize) himself and band members in a recording studio recording a song, hearing the event as it unfolds, and feeling what it might be like to be in that situation. The more detailed the vision, the better. If you have already experienced something in your mind, you can more readily create the circumstances to bring it about in actuality.

Clarity of vision is important because it significantly increases your chances of getting what you want. The problem with not being specific both about your vision and the planning process related to its achievement, is that you may get something you don't want. A while back, I was working as an education administrator in the field of higher education. At the time, I was undergoing a stressful period both at work and at home. I had become disenchanted with the organization I was working for, and had concerns regarding the ethics and qualifications of the leadership. At the same time, some personal issues cropped up at home and I wanted to dedicate more time to addressing them. While driving to work one morning, I was thinking about the day ahead while stopped at a stop sign near my home. At that moment I said aloud "I wish I had less responsibility. Even if it meant that I was earning (and then I said the salary aloud.)." The amount I stated was a little more than half of the salary I was earning at the time. Within a few weeks of my having uttered those words, I was advised of a restructure and was offered a position which paid exactly the salary amount I said to myself in the car a few weeks before. Thereafter, I was part of a layoff which took place a few months later. I recalled that the job had come to me in an unorthodox manner, and that when I accepted the job, I had decided that I would stay in it for at least two years and would then decide if I wanted to stay longer. The layoff occurred just after my two year anniversary with the company. In evaluating the event afterward, I realized that I did not follow the processes I had followed in the past and which are described in this book, for bringing about the change I wanted to see. At the time, I had no clear vision of what I wanted, nor a plan for achieving it. This is a perfect example of why what you think, what you say, and what you do, matters. Although I ultimately got what I wanted, it did not happen in the way I would have wanted. I was not clear about how I wanted to achieve the outcome. I left it to chance and had an experience that was less than desirable. In spite of this, however, the outcome had the effect it needed to have: it redirected my path. Without that experience I would not be doing what I am doing today: Living my passion.

CREATING A PLAN

Once you know what you want, using that information to set goals and to put a plan in place for achieving it is simple.

There are varying approaches to goal-setting and for developing plans of action. You may choose to focus on only one or a few specific goals, or you may choose to work toward more than one goal in areas of your life with which you are currently unhappy. You can begin by either creating a list of goals in order of priority, or you can identify goals within the five major areas of your life.

The first approach, where you make a list of things you want to accomplish, might initially look something like this:

- Train for and complete a triathlon
- Write and publish a book
- Perform for a live audience
- Earn a Masters degree
- Lose 30 pounds

The second approach revolves around identifying the areas of your life with which you are unhappy, and in which you would like to see changes. They include:

1. Health/Fitness
2. Financial
3. Career
4. Relationships
5. Spirituality

Each of these areas are rarely to our level of expectation or satisfaction all of the time, or all at the same time. Everyone pretty much knows which areas of their life are the problem areas at the moment, and in which they would like to make changes to meet their current expectations. For example, most people have specific health or fitness levels at which they want to or believe they should be. Their actual health and fitness levels do not match their ideal. This creates a mismatch between expectations and reality, and leads to dissatisfaction. In order to overcome being dissatisfied we have two choices:

1. Make changes that will get you to the level of your expectations, or

2. Change your goal/ideal in order to bridge the gap.

In other words, your choices are to change your current situation to meet your expectations, or accept your current situation, and modify your expectations.

As noted, the second option is really just a choice to change your expectations, whereas the first option requires you to make changes (and implement a plan) that will get you to the level of your expectations.

Whatever goals you set for yourself (either in the form of a prioritized list, or designated by areas of your life) you will need to clearly identify and prioritize those goals, and then implement a PLAN for each.

WRITING IT DOWN

Putting your goals in written form not only creates a record to which you can refer and review at any time, it also has the effect of transforming your goals into something tangible that you can see and touch. Committing your goals to paper helps to further strengthen your resolve to accomplishing them, but also serves to keep you on task.

EXERCISE – YOUR TURN

To begin the process of goal-setting and planning, follow these steps:

1. Create a sheet (electronic or handwritten) for each goal. Your goal should be specific and stated clearly in positive terms.

2. For each goal (sheet) create long-term milestones. Under each long-term milestone, add short-term milestones, which are steps that will lead to accomplishing each long-term milestone.

3. Under each short-term and long-term milestone, list the steps you will need to take to accomplish the specific milestone.

4. If you are unsure as to the steps you need to take to achieve the milestone and, ultimately, your goal, conduct internet research or find a mentor.

5. Using the information you included on each sheet, create a simple project plan to track your progress toward your goal. A project plan encapsulates all aspects of steps you need to take and tasks you need to complete to achieve short-term milestones, long-term milestones, and finally, your goal.

The goal worksheet can be in any format you choose, so long as the elements described are included. The next page has a sample of a simple worksheet format that I have used and which works for me. The example lists the ultimate goal, followed by long-term milestones needed to achieve the ultimate goal. Under each long-term milestone are short-term milestones or tasks which must be completed, in order to achieve each long-term goal. The idea is to keep the goals in mind, and to think through the steps you will need to take to achieve them.

SIMPLE GOAL WORKSHEET

GOAL	Long-Term Milestone	Short-Term Milestone	Target Date
Admission to Law School	Complete Undergraduate degree with honors.		6/30
	Take and Pass LSAT with score of 160 or better		4/31
		Enroll in LSAT Prep course	3/1
	Complete and submit applications to my top three choices for law schools		2/20
		Draft compelling personal statement for admission.	2/1

TIME LINE

Assigning due dates for completing tasks, milestones, and goals, is important. Deadlines truly help to keep us on task in moving toward the final outcome of our efforts. Dates should be realistic and should allow for any possible unforeseen delays.

EDITING AND REWORKING THE PLAN

As you move toward completing tasks, milestones, and goals, you may find the need to edit the milestone or goal, or the timelines associated with it. This is common and should not be considered a setback or obstacle. Indeed, you should expect to have to rework your plans on occasion. However, this should not deter you from continuing to pursue your dreams. In addition, you can adjust and adapt any of the recommended methods to fit your needs and preferences.

MY PLAN

As a writer, I regularly set goals related to my writing projects. I follow the process described above for identifying goals, identifying and setting short-term and long-term milestones, steps and tasks for reaching each milestone, and developing project plans. To give you an idea as to what a simple project plan might look like, a rough draft of my plan is included as a sample on the next page.

TAKING ACTION

Once you have identified goals, set milestones, and developed a plan, the next step is to take action. Although your plan may encompass more than one goal, you may want to choose the one that is most important to you and about which you are most passionate as a starting point. When and how often you act on the plan (or plans) you have developed will depend entirely on you. It is important to note, however, that making progress in completing tasks and milestones will not only move you closer to achieving your goal, but will help you to maintain focus and build momentum.

DECIDE

Before you go to the next page, decide to:

- Develop a plan based on a clear and precise vision of your goal(s).
- Follow the Plan and take action toward achieving your goal(s) on a regular basis.

SIMPLE PROJECT PLAN

Book Title	Tasks/Milestones	Due Date	Notes
The Five Decisions	Review and organize existing sections	4/25/2014	Ensure logical organization
	Edit and flesh out content	5/12/2014	
	Write new/additional content	5/18/2014	
	Incorporate personal experiences	5/25/2014	
	Finalize formatting and add index	5/30/2014	
	Conduct final REVIEW and EDITS	6/12-6/19/2014	
	Cover design – Meet with Espinoza Graphics	6/29/2014	Vacation 7/4 to 7/14
	Develop marketing campaign - to include website, blog, social networks		
	Submit to Kindle	7/15/2014	
	Determine best format for LSI Paperback	7/20/2014	
	Designer to design and submit cover to LSI	7/25/2014	
	Submit new title to LSI (Title set up process, etc.)	7/25/2014	
	Launch marketing campaign.	7/25/2014	

DECISION IV

DECIDE TO FOCUS

Chapter 6

THE POWER OF FOCUS

As you work toward achieving your goal(s) it is important to know that, of THE FIVE DECISIONS, the decision related to maintaining FOCUS is the most powerful.

As a strong believer that we are what we think, I know for certain that many of the things that I have thought about and focused my attention on in the past (both good and bad) have manifested themselves in my life. I also know that the things about which I am currently thinking and on which I am focusing my attention, will be my reality in the future.

Our ability to control where we focus our time and attention puts us in complete control. Failing to take advantage of that, results in our time and attention being drawn in several different directions. This is not productive, as two things may result: First, we delay the achievement of our goal(s). Second, we may focus time and attention on things we don't want, and thereby draw those things into our experience.

Focus refers to our ability to maintain our attention on the outcomes we wish to achieve, until we achieve them. Maintaining focus over the period of time it may take to achieve our goals may be challenging. There are, however, a variety of things we can do in order to help us maintain focus.

BEYOND BELIEF

Know that you will achieve your goal(s). Believing something will happen and knowing it will happen are two different things. As a starting point, it is critical that you not only believe in the goal(s) you have set, but that you <u>know</u> you will achieve them. Wanting something to happen, but not having complete faith that it will, impacts your commitment to and questions your ability to make it happen. Having complete faith that you will achieve your goals, however, leaves no room for doubt. Thus, it is important to squelch doubt when it arises and strengthen your resolve and commitment to seeing your goals realized. This is true even if you don't quite know how you are going to achieve them. Complete and unwavering faith can work wonders.

STAYING THE COURSE

As discussed in a prior chapter, goal setting is the means of clearly identifying your goals. We also addressed the importance of having a plan (and the process for developing a plan) for every goal you set. The Plan is essentially your blueprint for achieving your goal and sets forth long-term and short-term milestones toward your goal. The process of goal setting and planning not only provides direction, but in effect, helps you to stay focused on action steps in the form of milestones.

Given the number of daily activities or events that may distract us and thereby take our attention from our goals, there are steps we can take to ensure that we remain focused on and motivated to accomplish our goals. These include the use of :

- Visualization
- Motivational tools and techniques
- Gratitude

Whether you choose to review your goals daily, or engage in regular meditation and visualization exercises where you envision your goals as having been accomplished, you must take steps to stay focused on your goals. These actions will keep you from losing sight of the things you are striving to achieve, and will help you in identifying steps you can take toward making them happen. Each task or step associated with each milestone will enable you to remain focused on your goal(s).

A PRECONCEIVED OUTCOME (Visualization)

The saying "seeing is believing" means that a person cannot believe something exists until they see it with their own two eyes. What those people may fail to realize is that one can "see" not just with the eyes, but with the mind's eye. This is called visualization. Seeing something in your mind and "believing" it can exist, often leads to "seeing" something come to fruition in the physical world. The fact that something currently is not possible or does not exist does not mean that it won't ever be possible or won't ever exist. Phenomenal advancements have been made in our world due to the belief that, as Napoleon Hill so eloquently put it: "What the mind of man can conceive and believe, it can achieve." This same principle applies to the goals you set and want to achieve during your lifetime. Failing to use visualization as a means toward achieving your goals is to significantly limit yourself. Seeing yourself training for and completing the triathlon, preforming for a live audience, graduating with a Master's degree, or whatever your ultimate goal may be, is akin to aiming and throwing darts without a target board. In addition to solidifying the idea that your goal is possible, engaging in visualization exercises on a regular basis helps to keep your focus where it belongs: on achieving your goal.

MOTIVATION

If you are working toward a goal about which you are passionate, staying motivated and on track may not be an issue. This is especially true if it is a goal that can be accomplished over a short period of time. Often, however, life happens and we may begin to lose the enthusiasm we had at the time we started pursuing our goal(s). Not to worry. Motivational tools and techniques abound, from reading inspirational quotes, to forming your own support group or cheering section; they are too numerous to list here. You know yourself best and have likely already discovered the best methods to keep yourself motivated and thereby focused on your goal(s.) So choose whatever works best. Keep in mind that visualization (covered above) as well as practicing gratitude and journaling, which will be covered in the section and chapter that follow, are also great tools for reinvigorating your passion.

PRACTICING GRATITUDE

What are you thankful for? If this is a question you ponder only at Thanksgiving time, you are doing yourself a huge disservice. Taking a few minutes every day to think about and express gratitude for all that is wonderful about your life can have a huge impact on your attitude, state of mind, and on your perspective in dealing with the things that may not be so wonderful.

Do you have friends and family who are supportive and love you unconditionally? Do you have stable employment and work with colleagues you like being around? Do you have a home to go to and a car to drive? Do you have food to eat? Are you in reasonably good health? Do you love living in a country where you can have an opinion and the freedom to voice it? If you answered yes to any of these, recognize that many are not so fortunate.

All you have to do is look around to find things for which to be thankful. The clear blue sky, the fluffy white clouds, the rolling hills or mountains nearby, the radiant sun, the stars that sparkle – Thank God you have the eyes with which to see them. The birds that chirp, the child that laughs, the waves that crash – Thank God you have the ears with which to hear them. The hand that greets, your mother's hug, your child's face – Thank God that you can feel them. It is easy to get so wrapped up in the things that bother you that you fail to recognize the everyday beauty that surrounds you.

Being grateful and expressing gratitude for all you have in your life, including the things and people that surround you, will put you in a positive state of mind. When you focus on the good things in life, you are in a better position to bring about and to be open to receiving more of the things you want and accomplishing your goals.

What is beautiful about your life? Take time every day to acknowledge all that is good in your life - and you will know you have been blessed.

Engaging in daily activities which help us think about and take action toward our goals will ensure that our attention is in the right place. Similar to focusing the delicate lens of a camera on the amazing image we wish to capture, we must clearly focus our attention on the things we want to capture and to become part of our life experience. We must "zoom in" on the things we most want and keep our attention there until we get it.

In my own experience, the goals about which I was most passionate, dedicated to, and on which I consistently focused my thoughts and attention, were the goals I succeeded in accomplishing. Whether they were short-term or long-term goals, those I thought about frequently, meditated about, visualized and believed I would achieve, were the ones that have become my reality.

DECIDE:

Before you go to the next page, decide to:

- <u>Know</u> that you will succeed.
- Stay the course using visualization techniques, motivational tools, and by practicing gratitude.

DECISION V

DECIDE TO LET GO(D)

Chapter 7

LETTING GO(D)

"He who believes in me, believes not in me but in him who sent me."

~ John 12:44

As you move ahead toward accomplishing your goals, it is inevitable that you will encounter obstacles. Obstacles serve one of two purposes. One purpose is to test and strengthen our resolve, and the other is to redirect our path in the right direction. In order to ensure success you must determine the type and purpose of the obstacle so that you may overcome it. The means by which to overcome an obstacle which presents itself depends entirely on the obstacle. Obstacles tend to shift our focus away from our goal, may serve to weaken our determination, and threaten our perseverance. This prevents you from staying the course and, thereby, keeps you from your goal(s).

FORGIVENESS: A GIFT TO YOURSELF

Obstacles to success may not always come from outside forces. One possible obstacle to being successful is the inability to release past events and negative feelings associated with those events or people from our past. One way to overcome this obstacle is to practice forgiveness.

When you suffer emotional wounds due to the offensive words or actions of others, you may harbor the extremely negative emotions of fear, hatred, resentment and/or pain over an extended period of time. Each time you think about the event that caused you to feel that way, you re-experience it and it becomes a vicious cycle that can be burdensome. To relieve yourself of that burden, you must forgive.

Carrying hatred or harboring a grudge or ill feelings towards others puts you in a negative state of being. It is the equivalent of being imprisoned by the past and being held captive by old hurts and bad feelings. The energy used to sustain these negative feelings detracts from your ability to focus on the positive things you wish to create in life. By forgiving, you let go. To let something go, however, does not mean to condone or to forget the behavior that caused you to experience those negative emotions in the first place.

Forgiveness is a gift not just to the recipient of forgiveness, but to the person granting forgiveness. Forgiving another person truly is a precious gift you give to yourself. Letting go of those negative emotions by forgiving others is like opening the door to an emotional jail cell in which you have been imprisoned. By forgiving, you acknowledge that you have suffered enough and are ready to rise above the circumstances that resulted in the bad feelings. You can make room in your mind and in your heart for better things.

Life really is too short to spend it harboring ill feelings towards those who have wronged you. In the course of life, we all experience bad things in one way or another. Our time is better spent not bemoaning why it happened, but to glean whatever lesson we can from the event and then focus on the good things in our lives. Your ability, choice, and courage to forgive is to give to yourself the gift of freedom. Thus, learning to forgive is a gift only you can give yourself.

JOURNALING

Have you ever been so busy, confused, worried, angry or frustrated that you didn't know what to do next? If you answered "no," you are either not being honest or are suffering from short term memory loss. We all experience times like those mentioned above. It's nearly impossible not to if you lead a normal life. Times like these are a perfect time to step back, take a deep breath and whip out a pen and paper or find your trusty keyboard. Tranquility is just a few sentences (or paragraphs or pages) away. Journaling can help get you back on track when nothing else or nobody else can.

The relief you seek is at your fingertips. Journaling is a practice many engage in and for various reasons. The journaling of today is not your standard "Dear Diary, I had a great day at school today. Jim asked me to sit with him at lunch." Current day journaling can help to ease your worries, reduce stress, heal emotional wounds, and may serve as a playbook for your future success.

In a previous chapter we discussed the negative impact of worry. To worry is to fear the worst and to expect the worst. It is, in effect, to give up on God. In addition to the techniques addressed previously for eradicating worry, you can use journaling as a tool to relieve the burden brought on by worrying.

Worry is like a weight we carry around with us. It detracts from our ability to live in the moment. The same can be said of anger and frustration. By pouring your worries onto the page and working through worst case scenarios, you can establish a plan of action and move on with your life without the fear of the unknown. If the worst does happen, you, at the very least, have a plan.

Through writing, you gain a better perspective on how you feel and why you feel that way. It's an opportunity to explore your feelings regarding events, situations, and relationships.

Journaling enables you to examine and re-evaluate personal and professional goals. It can also be the perfect place to document your plans as to next steps that will help you achieve the success you are after. Another benefit of journaling is that it is also a great way to capture your history in writing. Your journal, documenting important events in your lifetime, may become a treasured family keepsake that will serve as a window on the past to future generations. As such, it may also serve as a source for your future memoir.

Writing in a journal is popular for a reason. Those who use a journal on a regular basis can attest to it's therapeutic effects. So the next time you are so busy, confused, worried, angry or frustrated you don't know what to do next, you'll know what to do next. Here's to your peace of mind.

CONSIDER GOD

If you believe in God, it is important to remember the greatness of God when obstacles present themselves. When issues arise that prevent us from accomplishing those things we are trying to accomplish, we may tend to focus on the problem and feel defeated and deflated, instead of managing our perspective. It is often said that everything happens for a reason. I like to think that everything that happens, happens for a good reason. This means that although the issue or event may seem problematic at the time, it will ultimately serve a beneficial purpose. Therefore, in spite of whatever obstacles or limitations you may encounter on your path to achieving your goals, remember that, with God, anything is possible.

DECIDE

Before you go to the next page, decide to:

- Forgive yourself and others.

- Use journaling as a tool to overcome obstacles.
- Consider the greatness of God.

Chapter 8

NO FEAR

What do you want to be when you grow up? I remember being asked this question many times over the course of my childhood. I answered that question with no hesitation and great conviction. I am going to be a ballerina, I said confidently. It was what I wanted and I had no doubt that I would achieve it.

We are all that way as children. We are brimming with confidence and believe we can do anything without limitation. We had great imaginations and used them to the fullest extent. I know I was that way, and I have witnessed it also in my own children. I remember when my son, a toddler at the time, decided he not only could, but would, climb up on the dining room chair, followed by the table, so that he could swing the light fixture back and forth for his amusement. I promptly plucked him off the table before he suffered what I thought could be a serious injury if he happened to fall. I remember thinking that he had no fear. He set his mind on what he wanted to do, he decided how to go about it; then, he did it. There was no hesitation, no doubts or second thoughts. He just did it. No fear. During that time, and in the years that followed, I would explain to my son and daughter, how dangerous it is to climb things (i.e. a table, a ladder, a tree, etc.) The risk of falling was too great and I did not want them to fall and injure themselves. These, of course, were just a few of the many things I cautioned them against doing over the years. Although I may have saved both from a few bruises and possibly a broken limb, it made me think about the possible lifelong impact of putting fear into their minds. Would discouraging them from climbing a chair or table prevent them from climbing to new heights in future endeavors? Would they question their abilities to accomplish something, or even decide not to take action because of the possible risks?

As you may have surmised, I did not grow up to be a ballerina. As is known to happen, my career goals changed over the years. I studied law and became licensed to practice, but chose instead to enter the field of higher education administration, and later to pursue a writing career. In thinking about how or why my goals changed, I can't help but think of the cautionary advice I received or of comments made by well-intentioned parents, teachers, counselors, and friends. I learned that girls who become ballerinas are typically tall, thin, and beautiful, and they can afford to take dance lessons for years on end. They have natural dance ability and are also graceful. Perhaps, in the eyes of others or in my own eyes, I wasn't many of these things, or even any of them. I don't remember the reason, but at some point I moved on to new dreams of what I wanted to be when I grew up – a dancer, a singer, and finally, in high school, I decided I wanted to be a lawyer. I decided this after completing a "career choice" research paper as part of a high school English assignment and presentation. Up until that point in time, I had been undecided as to what career I wanted to pursue, and my dreams of being a dancer or any of the other things I dreamed about had long disappeared. I knew I was going to go to college, as my parents had always emphasized the importance of a good education. The research I conducted for the class assignment helped to guide my decision.

This brings to mind the middle-aged, male, high-school counselor who, when I said I wanted to go to law school after college, encouraged me to, instead, go to a career college and become a secretary. Why, I wondered, did he suggest that? What was his reason and purpose? Were my grades not good enough? Perhaps he did not think I was sufficiently intelligent. Was it because of my ethnicity or gender? I would never know. Although his comments shattered my confidence initially, his words also had another impact. They lit a fire in me that would make me push through even the most difficult days while working and going to college. I'll show him, I thought. Well, I did show him, figuratively speaking. His words, though hurtful at the time, made me realize that I could accomplish anything I wanted to accomplish, regardless of what others say or think. I discovered that with passion, a clear vision of what I wanted to accomplish, goals, an action plan, focused effort, and a lot of faith, I could do it. I also learned that fear of risks and self-doubt go a long way in preventing us from pursuing our passions.

I have since tried to communicate to my children that they are fully capable of accomplishing whatever it is they wish to pursue. I have been trying to somehow undo any possible damage caused by my own well intentioned comments from the past. Recently, a conversation with my son, now a teenager, presented an opportunity to discuss limitations, as well as innovation. We had just returned from a trip to visit my parents in the Tucson area. I was unpacking my bag, when he walked in to my room and began a conversation with me. Whatever it was that was the topic of discussion prompted me to remind him: "Now, remember," I said. "Anything you want to do in life, whatever it may be, is possible. You can do it if you just put forth the effort." He replied: "You can't fly." I was both amused and taken aback at his response. He had a point. I said – "Well, you may not have the wings with which to fly, but people who wanted to fly, in spite of not having wings, put the effort forth and figured out a way to do so." This, of course, is called innovation. Innovation is a means of getting around limitations.

81

CONCLUSION

Chapter 9

HE ASKED, I ANSWERED

In thinking back to that day I went to the chapel, and recalling the event that occurred in mere seconds, I realize that things have finally come full circle. The lesson to be learned that day has, in the process of writing this book, become crystal clear. We serve God by serving others.

I am grateful that my friend invited me to accompany her to the chapel that day. Thankfully, her heart condition was successfully treated without further incident and she lives a happy life surrounded by her loved ones.

I am not certain as to what prompted me to ask those questions that day. I am, however, certain of one thing: I found my purpose.

DECIDE

Before moving forward, decide to commit to THE FIVE DECISIONS.

I. Decide that you are responsible and in control.

II. Decide on precisely what you want.

III. Decide to plan and take action.

IV. Decide to focus.

V. Decide to let Go(d).

www.ingramcontent.com/pod-product-compliance
Lightning Source LLC
Chambersburg PA
CBHW031341040426
42443CB00006B/429